Different Like Me

My Book of Autism Heroes

Jennifer Elder

Illustrated by Marc Thomas and Jennifer Elder

Jessica Kingsley *Publishers*
London and Philadelphia

First published in 2006
by Jessica Kingsley Publishers
73 Collier Street
London N1 9BE, UK
and
400 Market Street, Suite 400
Philadelphia, PA 19106, USA

www.jkp.com

Library of Congress Cataloging in Publication Data
Elder, Jennifer, 1968-
    Different like me : my book of autism heroes / Jennifer Elder ; illustrations by Marc
Thomas and Jennifer Elder.
        p. cm.
    ISBN-13: 978-1-84310-815-3 (hardback : alk. paper)
    ISBN-10: 1-84310-815-1 (hardback : alk. paper) 1. Autism—Juvenile literature. 2.
Celebrities—Juvenile literature. I. Thomas, Marc. II. Title.
    RC553.A88E43 2005
    618.92'85882—dc22
                                                        2005014169

British Library Cataloguing in Publication Data
A CIP catalogue record for this book is available from the British Library

ISBN 978 1 84310 815 3
eISBN 978 0 85700 705 6

Printed and bound in China

For Morgan and Bramwell

❧ About Me ❧

Hello! My name is Quinn. I'm eight and three-quarters years old. My favorite things are baseball, dolphins, and ancient Egypt. Oh yeah, and I'm autistic. Sometimes I don't understand people, and sometimes they don't understand me. Little things get on my nerves, like too many people talking at once. It can be hard to fit in. But when the other kids see how good I am at drawing, they are interested. This is how I make my place in the world. I just concentrate on what I do best.

Did you know that nobody had ever even heard of autism until the 1940s? It was around before then, but there just wasn't a name for it yet. Then two different doctors, Dr. Kanner and Dr. Asperger, each started thinking about what some of their patients had in common. Some didn't speak. Some were very good with numbers and patterns. Some were bothered by loud noises. But they all seemed to live in a world of their own, hardly noticing people around them. Both of these doctors, thousands of miles apart, looked at their patients and came up with the same word: Autism (from the Greek word for "self").

Still, it took a long time for us to begin to understand autism. It wasn't until forty years later that Dr. Asperger's work became widely known. Since the beginning of the twenty-first century, we have learned much more about autism and Asperger's Syndrome in the Arts and Sciences—some who blend in with the crowd, and some who proudly let it show.

Sometimes I wonder about all the autistic people who lived before, though. Most probably never met anyone else like them. They must have thought that they were the only ones who ever cared more about trains, or music, or the planets, than about making friends. They probably assumed that every person on earth but them knew the secret to fitting in. Did they wonder why they weren't like everybody else? And how did they turn their unique abilities into something great? It's hard to say for sure, but there are even some famous people who I think may have been different like me…

❦ Albert Einstein ❧

Albert Einstein was not a boy genius—at least, not as far as anyone knew. Most people thought that he wasn't very smart. He didn't talk at all until the age of three, and still didn't speak well when he reached the age of nine. About the only thing he was good at was playing the violin. Albert didn't do well in school, and his teachers were often irritated with him. One school even threw him out. They thought he was hopeless.

They were wrong.

There was something going on inside Albert's head, something wonderful. The first time Albert saw a compass, when he was around age five, he was fascinated. What made the needle move? How did it know which way to point? These questions, along with his love of math, would eventually lead young Albert to the science of physics.

After college, Albert took a job in a patent office. He never stopped thinking about physics, though, and began to write his ideas about time and space. Then, in 1905, he published a paper that shook the world. When people read what he wrote, they were amazed. Some of it was hard to understand; he predicted that time could slow as you approached the speed of light and that space itself could be pulled out of shape. He even showed that anything—a jellybean, a lump of metal, a drop of water—held immense energy inside of it. His ideas took years for other scientists to prove, but one thing was always certain: Einstein's work would change everything. Albert became very famous. He traveled all over, lecturing and teaching—even at the college where he had been a poor student.

Some of Albert's ideas were used to build the atomic bomb, the biggest weapon ever made. This made Albert sad, because he was a pacifist—someone who is against war. He spent the rest of his life trying to convince countries not to use the bomb. For this reason, he is remembered not just as a great scientist, but as a great man as well.

ℭ Dian Fossey ℬ

Dian Fossey was a lonely child, always longing for the one thing she wasn't allowed to have: a pet. She was awkward around other children, and yearned for companionship. Then, as a young woman, Dian's life changed when she read a book about zoology, the study of animals. She was inspired by this book to take a trip to Africa. Dian traveled to many countries, and met Dr. Louis Leakey, a famous scientist. Best of all, she saw lots of animals. Dian loved Africa and was sad to leave it when it was time to go home.

Dr. Leakey remembered the tall, shy young woman and helped her return to Africa to study gorillas in 1966. Dian set up camp on a mountain in the country of Rwanda. It was not easy to get to. The nearest trail a car could drive on was three miles away. From there you had to hike, carrying whatever you needed up the side of the mountain. That didn't stop Dian, though. Soon she had a metal hut built for herself, a hut for guests, and several other structures.

It was difficult to get close to the gorillas. They were wild animals, after all. Dian decided that she would watch what the gorillas did and try to act like a gorilla. She walked like a gorilla, she ate like a gorilla, and she made noises like a gorilla. Little by little, the gorillas got used to her.

Over her 18 years in Rwanda, Dian became very attached to the gorillas. She gave them names and called them her friends. Dian did not get along well with other humans, though. Some local people saw her as an outsider and thought she should go back home. Dian had problems both with poachers—who killed gorillas, or sold them to zoos—and with farmers, who cut down forests where the gorillas lived.

Because of Dian Fossey's work, we know much more than we did about gorillas. But Dian did more than just watch the gorillas. She also made people aware of how important it was to save them. Thanks to Dian, today there are people all over the world working to help gorillas survive in the wild.

❧ Andy Warhol ❧

Before he was famous, Andy Warhol worked as a commercial artist, drawing pictures of things to help stores sell them. When Andy decided to make his own art, he still painted the same sorts of things, like soup cans and soda bottles. This was called "Pop Art," art inspired by advertising, TV, and comic books. Andy painted these things over and over and over again.

Andy's prints and paintings became very popular in the 1960s. Everybody wanted one of his works, and they were selling faster than he could make them. So Andy got some other artists to help him, and they worked together in a large studio called The Factory. They also made music at The Factory, and very long movies. One movie shows a man sleeping. Another is just one long shot of the Empire State building that goes on for eight hours. Not many people have ever watched the whole thing!

Andy started meeting lots of famous people and making portraits of them. These prints made people look strange—with pink eyes or blue lips—but they were a big hit. Andy became very rich, and one thing he used his money for was collecting. When Andy found something he liked, such as a cookie jar, he would buy as many of them as he could. Like Andy's art, collections are the same thing over and over again.

Even in the New York art world, at the center of a whole scene that he created, Andy remained the same shy, quiet person he had always been. He lived with his mother and basically kept to himself. There are lots of pictures of Andy at fancy New York parties. But when you look at his face in these pictures, it's hard to tell whether he's having a good time or whether he'd rather be back at home making art.

Andy is still interesting today because he was many things at once. He was a shy, quiet person but had lots of friends and went to parties. He didn't like to be interviewed but started a magazine called *Interview*. His art was funny and sad and deep and empty, all at the same time. Even his friends felt they didn't know him well. Andy once said that in the future, everybody will be famous for 15 minutes. That may be true for other people, but Andy Warhol will be famous for a long, long time.

ଓଃ Benjamin Banneker ଚ

Benjamin Banneker's grandmother was from England, and his grandfather was from Africa. In the 1700s in America, there were laws against people of different colors getting married. They got married anyway, though, and lived out in the country where nobody would bother them.

The Banneker family farm was far from town, so Benjamin's grandmother taught the children at home. Then, when Benjamin was 12, a school for boys opened nearby. Benjamin was excited about going to school, and he was a brilliant student. In fact, he learned so fast that soon he knew more about math than the teacher did!

When Benjamin was 21, he was given a pocket watch. After taking the watch apart and putting it back together, Benjamin decided to make his own clock out of wood. The wooden clock kept good time for 40 years. It is said to be the first clock made in America.

Later, after reading a book on astronomy, Benjamin built a "work cabin" on his land. Neighbors were used to seeing him lying on his back, looking at the stars. Now he had a skylight to look through and a telescope. He used his math skills to predict many events, including a solar eclipse. Other astronomers thought it would be on a different day, but Benjamin saw that they had made a mistake. The eclipse took place on April 14 1789, just as Benjamin had predicted.

Benjamin loved science and math, but he realized that other things were important too. The books that he wrote included ideas about peace and freedom. He was proud to be an American, and proud of his African heritage. The fight against slavery was very important to him. Benjamin was a free man, but his father and grandfather had both been slaves. He had learned from them what a terrible thing slavery was. Benjamin even exchanged letters with Thomas Jefferson on the subject, hoping to change the future president's mind.

Today, we know Benjamin Banneker as the first African-American scientist. In his own time, though, he was known by a more colorful name: The Sable Genius.

❧ Andy Kaufman ❧

Andy Kaufman was a comedian—only, not everyone thought that he was funny. In fact, not even Andy thought he was funny. He wanted to entertain people, but he didn't tell jokes. Andy did strange things, and people laughed…or they didn't. Mostly, he seemed to want to watch people's reactions, like someone from another planet studying human life. At one show he took the whole audience out for milk and cookies. Was that a funny thing to do? Or just interesting? Or neither one?

On television, Andy played a number of different characters. One was a famous singer. Another was a showbiz guy with a wig and a cigar. On the show *Taxi*, he played a shy mechanic from another country. This was probably closest to the real Andy. The shy mechanic sometimes forgot who he was and turned into a supercool guy, the opposite of his own personality. This was a little bit like shy Andy turning into a different person as an actor.

Andy's humor was often about what made people uncomfortable. At that time, women were finally gaining equal rights in work, school, and family life. A few years before, in the 1970s, a woman had beaten a man in a famous tennis match. Andy thought it might be funny to challenge women to wrestling contests. This didn't seem fair because Andy was bigger than most of the women he wrestled. Some people thought this was mean; others thought it was funny. Some didn't know what to think. At one match, Andy got hurt and had to be taken away in an ambulance. Many people thought he was just faking, that it was all part of his show.

Years later, people are still talking about Andy Kaufman. A song and a movie were made about him, both called *Man on the Moon*. There were people who didn't believe that anybody ever really went to the moon, because they couldn't see it with their own eyes. In a way, it was the same with Andy. Sometimes, it was hard to tell if he was being real, or just kidding. Only Andy knew for sure.

∝ Wassily Kandinsky ∾

As a boy, in the 1870s, Wassily Kandinsky would visit the museums of Moscow with his parents. Later, he would make copies of the paintings he had seen from memory. Wassily also wrote poems and played piano and cello. Everyone agreed that he was very talented. Instead of studying art, though, Wassily grew up to be a lawyer. But there was always art inside of him, trying to get out.

Then, one day, Wassily saw an art show that opened his eyes. It was an exhibit of Impressionist paintings. The Impressionists used wild brush strokes, something people had not seen before. Wassily was very excited about this. He quit his job and became an artist.

Wassily was a very good painter. He was inspired by folk art and made colorful paintings of people, horses, and landscapes. Still, he wasn't satisfied. Painting horses was OK, but Wassily wanted something more. He wanted to paint feelings. He wanted to paint sounds. Wassily was a synaesthete.

A "synaesthete" is someone who hears colors, or smells music. This sounds silly, but everyone does it sometimes. That's why you might think that red candy tastes better than blue candy, even if they're exactly the same flavor. This happens to a synaesthete all day long. Every time the phone rings, it smells like flowers or feels like sandpaper to them.

To Wassily, every musical instrument had a color. A trumpet sound was yellow. The flute was blue. A tuba was bright red. When he put many different colors in the same painting, it was like an orchestra playing. The problem with being a synaesthete, though, is that not everyone sees things the same way you do. Wassily saw music in his paintings; most other people just saw squiggly lines and colors. Those people called Wassily's art "abstract"—art that is not a picture of anything.

Today, abstract art is everywhere. In Wassily Kandinsky's time, though, people found it shocking. They were happy with pictures of things they could see, like trees and flowers. This new art was confusing: What did it mean? What was it about? If you didn't like it, was it because it wasn't good, or because you just didn't get it? Now we look at Wassily's art, and all the abstract art that came after it, with new eyes. Sometimes art that's about things you can't see can be the most interesting art of all.

Julia Bowman Robinson

The first thing Julia Bowman could remember doing was sitting on the ground, lining up pebbles. To Julia, they were more than pretty patterns. They were the beginnings of her lifelong love of numbers. Julia was slow to speak and very shy. When she came down with a terrible fever and had to stay home from school, her parents worried that she would fall behind. Instead, over the two years she missed, Julia completed almost four years of class work.

When she went back to school, Julia was the only 12-year-old in the ninth grade. This made her even more timid. She ate lunch in a corner, as fast as she could. Then, one day, a girl named Virginia invited Julia to eat lunch with her. Virginia was as good at art as Julia was at math. The two girls became best friends, and Julia came out of her shell. It didn't matter anymore that she was the only girl in her math class, the only girl in physics. Julia didn't pay any attention to what girls were or weren't supposed to do. In the 1930s baseball was for boys, but Julia was an avid fan. She spent all her money on sports magazines, went to baseball games, and kept detailed records of the scores.

In college, Julia took a class in a branch of mathematics called number theory. It was a hard class; by the end of the year there were only four students left. But Julia was hooked. Number theory reminded her of the pebbles from her childhood. She felt that this was what she was always meant to do.

Julia became a very successful mathematician. She worked for large companies and taught college classes. She was honored with many awards. Still, one thing made Julia sad. She loved bicycles, but her childhood illness had left her too weak to ride. Then, when she was 41, Julia had an operation on her heart. After that, she could ride as much as she wanted. Julia was overjoyed. She took long trips across America and Holland. Julia felt free.

Over the years, there was one math problem Julia could not solve. It was called "Hilbert's Tenth." Of course, nobody else could solve it either, but Julia knew it was possible. Julia thought about it for 20 years. She thought about it while she worked. She thought about it while she rode her bike. She thought about it while she ate her lunch. Julia had solved the whole thing, except for one little piece. Then, one day, she heard that a young man in Russia had found the missing piece. "Hilbert's Tenth" was solved. You might think that after working on the problem for so long, Julia would be upset that she couldn't solve it on her own. But she was happy. Julia said that for all those years she was just waiting for that young man to grow, so he could help her.

❧ Piet Mondrian ❧

Artists are messy, right? They get paint on their clothes, paint in their hair, and paint on the floor. Well, maybe some artists, but not Piet Mondrian. Piet worked in a clean, empty room, with no decorations and nothing to distract him. He had a wooden crate to sit on and a record player, and that was it. Piet was neat.

In Holland, where Piet was from, artists painted landscapes. Piet painted landscapes, too. But the more he painted, the more he wondered: Is that flower pretty because it is a flower, or because of its shape and color? Why not just paint the shape? Or the color? Piet started to look at everything in a new way. Houses were squares. Clouds were blobs. The ocean was made of blue dots. Soon, his paintings didn't look like pictures of anything. They were just shapes.

Piet wasn't the only artist painting shapes. There were others who thought it was a good idea, too. Not only were their shapes good for paintings, but for sculptures, buildings, even whole cities. Piet and the other artists started a magazine about it called *The Style*. Many artists and designers were inspired by *The Style*. Today you can still find this look in lots of places, from office buildings to clothing stores. There is even a chain of hot dog stands inspired by *The Style*.

For Piet, though, it was about more than just how things looked. Piet lived through two world wars and thought the world was a mess. He wanted his art to be something neat, clean, and perfect. So Piet made some rules. His paintings would be flat and smooth, white with black lines, and three colors: red, blue, and yellow. The only shapes in his paintings would be squares and rectangles. Piet stuck to these rules for years. He was so sure of them that when another artist added diagonal lines to *The Style*, Piet quit the magazine in disgust.

In 1940, a bomb exploded near where Piet was living in London. Piet was sick of war. He moved far away from it all, to New York. Suddenly, there were bright lights, color, and jazz music all around him. Piet began to see that there could be more than just red, blue, and yellow. He started breaking his own rules, painting colorful, happy pictures. Piet painted one of his most famous paintings there, and even the title tells you how he felt about New York: *Broadway Boogie Woogie*.

᎒ Alan Turing ᎒

Autistic people like computers. Autistic people are good with computers. But did you know that an autistic person invented the computer? Well, actually, it took a lot of people to invent the computer, over many years. One man, though, was so important that we call him "The Father of Modern Computing."

Alan Turing's parents lived in India, but they sent Alan to England for boarding school. Alan was very lonely and unhappy at school. He struggled in English class and had terrible handwriting. Still, he did very well in math and science and went on to Cambridge University. It was there that Alan wrote a very important paper.

"On Computable Numbers" was about a machine that could do math. Of course there are lots of machines that can do math now, but back then it was just an idea. In fact, the word "computer" didn't use to mean a machine at all. It meant a person who did math. When someone needed a hard math problem solved, they would have many human "computers" work on it together. Nobody had come up with a machine that could do math as well as people could. Alan figured out that you needed to tell a machine what to do—to "program" it. His idea of a computer is now called "The Turing Machine."

Alan's work was interrupted by World War II. The British government needed someone to read messages for them. These weren't just any messages; they were secret messages, written in code. Nobody could figure them out. So the government brought together the smartest people they could find to break the code. Finally, they solved it and built a machine called the Colossus to translate the secret messages.

After the war, Alan went to work building giant computers. He programmed them to do everything from playing chess to designing airplanes. As time went by, he got more and more interested in "artificial intelligence," or AI. AI is the idea of a computer that can think like a person. Alan came up with "The Turing Test": whether a computer could fool someone into thinking it was a human being. As far as we know, it hasn't happened yet. Some say it never will. But Alan believed it could.

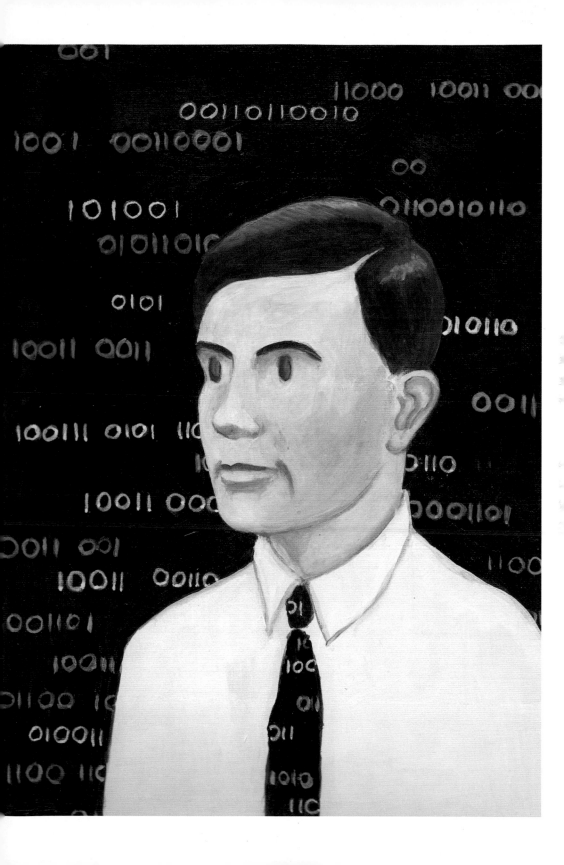

✂ Sophie Germain ✄

In Sophie Germain's time, math was for men. Some people worried that if girls learned math they would spend all their time thinking, instead of doing housework. Others didn't think girls could even understand math. This sounds crazy now, but it's what people thought for thousands of years.

Sophie wasn't just any girl, though. She was very smart, and very stubborn. When Sophie was 13 the French Revolution broke out. Rich people and poor people fought over who would rule the country, and soon the different sides began fighting among themselves too. It was a confusing and dangerous time, and there was danger on the streets of Paris, where Sophie lived. Sophie's parents decided that she'd better stay inside for a while, until it was all over.

So Sophie was stuck in the house with nothing to do. Nothing to do but read, that is. That was OK with Sophie, because she loved to read. She spent hours in her father's library, going through the books. Then, one day, she read about a mathematician named Archimedes. Sophie was thrilled. Suddenly, math was all she wanted to do. She read every math book she could find and stayed up late into the night, solving problems. Her parents didn't like it. Each night they would snuff all the candles and put out the fire so it would be too dark and cold for Sophie to stay up. They even took away her clothes so she would stay in bed! But Sophie was hard-headed. She would hide a candle, and as soon as everyone was asleep she would wrap herself in a quilt, light the candle, and work on her math. Nobody knew, until one morning when they found Sophie asleep at her desk, her cheek resting on a page full of numbers.

Over time, Sophie studied hard and gained the respect of other mathematicians. But it was still hard to be a woman in a man's world. Sophie wanted to discuss her work with a famous mathematician, Carl Gauss. She wrote him a letter, but signed it "Mr. LeBlanc." They wrote back and forth for years. Carl always believed that Sophie was a man. She was worried that if he knew she was a woman, he would not take her seriously. Finally, though, Carl found out by accident. Instead of being angry with Sophie for tricking him, Carl became Sophie's best friend, helping her in any way he could.

Sophie won prizes for her work and was awarded an honorary doctorate from the university where Carl Gauss taught. But the most impressive result of Sophie's work did not happen until many years later. Thanks to discoveries that Sophie made, engineers were able to dream up one of the greatest structures in the world. Today, the Eiffel Tower is the symbol of Paris, the city of Sophie Germain.

☙ Lewis Carroll ❧

Once upon a time there were two men: a very serious professor named Charles Dodgson, who wrote math books, and a silly man named Lewis Carroll, who made up puzzles and told funny stories. As different as they were, though, they had a few things in common. They came from the same town. They wore the same clothes. They even used the same toothbrush. In fact, they were the same person.

Charles Dodgson had a happy childhood until he went off to boarding school. He felt very homesick there. The other boys made fun of his stutter, which only made it worse. Two things got Charles through this difficult time: memories of home and math. Later, after graduating from Oxford, Charles was offered a job there teaching math. There was a catch, though: the job was open only to a bachelor—a man who doesn't have a wife or children. Charles took the job, knowing that it meant he would never have a family of his own.

Making friends was always difficult for Charles. He had a hard time even speaking to other adults. Around children, he was more relaxed. One day, on a picnic, the children begged Charles to tell them a story. He told them a tale about a girl named Alice—which just happened to be the name of one of the little girls at the party. The story was a big hit with the kids. When Charles got home, he decided to write it all down. In 1865, the story became a book called *Alice's Adventures in Wonderland*. Of course, people knew Charles Dodgson as a stuffy math professor, which didn't quite go with this very unstuffy book. So he decided that he needed a different name for the book cover—a pen name. The name he came up with, Lewis Carroll, is how most people know him today.

Alice's Adventures in Wonderland was so popular that Charles was inspired to write another book: *Through the Looking Glass and What Alice Found There*. Some people like that one even better than the first. Both had something that all the best kid's books share: They were as fun for grown-ups as they were for kids. Parents didn't get bored reading Alice books over and over again. Some adults even bought the books for themselves! Today, these books have been translated into more than 30 languages, including Spanish, Japanese, and Arabic.

Isaac Newton

In 1665, when Isaac Newton was at Cambridge University, something very bad happened. A terrible disease swept across England. It was not safe to be in the city, where healthy people were crowded together with the sick. So Isaac had to go back to his family's farm. Now, Isaac was very smart, but he was a useless farmer. His mother knew this and just let him do what he wanted all day.

And what Isaac wanted to do was think. Isaac was an amazing thinker. According to Isaac, what made him different from other people was that he could concentrate on one thing and never stop thinking about it until the thinking was done. He thought about light. He thought about colors. He thought about numbers. He even thought about what made things stay attached to the ground instead of flying off into space. Why does an apple fall down from the tree, instead of up? He thought and thought until the answer came to him. Isaac had discovered gravity, the force that pulls little things—like apples—to big things—like the earth.

Another thing Isaac discovered was how to make a better telescope. He showed his telescope to some very smart people, and they loved it. So Isaac shared more things, like his ideas about light and color. But not everyone agreed with Isaac's ideas, and that hurt his feelings. He decided to keep the rest of his ideas to himself.

Many years went by. Isaac did lots of important things, like teaching at Cambridge University, but he didn't share his discoveries with anyone. They weren't a secret, exactly; he just didn't know how important they were. Luckily, somebody else did. When Isaac's friend Edmund Halley asked him about gravity, Isaac dug up what he had written long ago. Edmund was amazed at Isaac's discoveries. Isaac wasn't sure about sharing them with other people, but Edmund kept bugging and bugging him until he agreed. Edmund helped Isaac turn his ideas into books that changed the way people thought forever.

One thing Isaac had come up with all those years before was a new kind of math called "calculus." But before Isaac could get around to telling anybody about it, somebody else thought of it too! So who invented calculus? Isaac, who thought of it first? Or the other guy, who told people first? Believe it or not, people argued about this for over a hundred years. Some people still don't agree. But it doesn't really matter. Either way, Isaac Newton is one of the greatest scientists in history.

☙ Nikola Tesla ❧

Nikola Tesla had a brilliant imagination. Before he built a machine, he would picture it in his mind. Then he would turn it on, test it, and fix any problems—all in his head! He came up with all sorts of things this way. Many museums still have "Tesla coils" on display—generators that shoot out bright ribbons of electricity.

When Nikola was a young man, in the 1880s, people were just learning how to use electricity. Nikola believed that something called "alternating current," or AC, was the answer to some electrical problems. But Nikola's boss, the inventor Thomas Edison, believed in "direct current," or DC. This was not the only thing Nikola and Thomas disagreed on. Nikola thought Thomas was a slob. Thomas thought Nikola was a pain. Nikola said Thomas owed him $50,000. Thomas said he didn't. Nikola quit. Good riddance, said Thomas.

What Thomas didn't realize was that Nikola was right. AC really was the answer. One thing AC could do was make electricity travel farther. This is important, because if the lights go out in your town, you might need to get power from another town. The electricity might have to travel for hundreds of miles. Nikola made that possible.

As much as Nikola loved science, he loved birds even more. On his walks around New York, Nikola would pick up sick or injured pigeons and bring them home. Soon he had a whole flock. This would have been OK in a house with a yard, but Nikola lived in a hotel. The people who worked there weren't too happy about the pigeons. Still, Nikola was a great man, so they put up with it. One man who knew Nikola described finding him so covered in birds that all he could see were Nikola's shiny leather shoes.

People remember Nikola both for his great inventions and his unique personality. He was always dressed up in formal clothes, even in the laboratory; but he couldn't stand jewelry, especially pearls. Nikola loved the darkness, hated germs, and was obsessed with the number three. For a long time, he ate nothing but milk and crackers. Because of his strange genius, Nikola had many fans. Some thought that he could predict the future, or talk to aliens. Nikola never claimed any of those things, but he did have ideas that seemed crazy back then. Now we know that his ideas were just ahead of their time.

ೞ Paul Erdös ๛

How would you like a guest who never cleaned up after himself? What if you had to wash his clothes, cook his dinner, and make his bed? Well, that's the kind of guest Paul Erdös was. Some people said he didn't know how to do these things, because his parents didn't even let him butter his own toast. Other people said he was just too busy thinking. Either way, the people Paul stayed with had to do everything for him, from picking him up at the airport to shining his shoes. They were happy to do it, because it was such an honor to have him visit. They even paid him!

Of course, people didn't pay Paul to mess up their houses. They paid him to do math. Paul's mind was like the most wonderful math book ever written—only better, because it was always growing and changing. In the 1960s and 1970s, Paul flew all over the world, talking to people about math. There was a long waiting list of schools and companies that wanted him. If you had a question about math, Paul was the person to ask.

People did lots of things for Paul, but he also did things for other people. Paul was very nice to young mathematicians. He would offer them money to solve math problems, sometimes as much as $3000. He also set up prizes for math students in Hungary, where he was born, and Israel, where he later lived. Although Paul was not a rich man, he shared whatever he had. A mathematician who Paul admired lived in India. Unfortunately, they never had a chance to meet. But whenever Paul gave a speech in India, he would give whatever money he earned to the Indian mathematician's family.

Paul Erdös was once called "the man who loved only numbers." It's easy to see why—he traveled so much that he was never home and didn't have time for much else. But there were other things that Paul liked to do. He enjoyed walking, climbing, and telling jokes. Like many mathematicians, he played chess and Go, as well as ping pong. But what Paul Erdös really loved was sharing ideas with other people. At each new place, he would begin his visit by saying, "My mind is open."

☙ Glenn Gould ❧

Glenn Gould hated the sound of clapping. He also hated dressing up and being watched. Unfortunately, when your job is playing piano on stage, you have to put up with all three of those things. So Glenn, the most popular pianist in the world, just quit. It wasn't an easy decision to make. The piano was Glenn's life. He had been reading music since he was three and performing in public since he was 12. But in 1964, when he was 32, Glenn decided that he had had enough.

So, if he wasn't going to give concerts, what was he going to do? Glenn decided to spend his time recording. He already had one bestselling album, but there was a lot more music that Glenn wanted to record. Some pieces that were too quiet for a noisy concert hall worked perfectly in the silent recording studio. Of course, you could hear *everything* in the silence, including the sound of Glenn humming as he played. But Glenn's playing was so magical that nobody minded the humming.

Glenn's favorite sort of music had "counterpoint"—more than one tune playing at the same time. He thought that counterpoint might also work in other kinds of art. Glenn interviewed people for a radio program, then edited the voices together to sound like they were having a conversation, or all talking at the same time. The result was a sort of talking music.

Some people who met Glenn thought he was a bit odd. For one thing, he did not like to shake hands. There was a good reason for that, though: Someone had once hurt his hand by shaking it too hard, and he worried that if his hand was hurt, he wouldn't be able to play. Glenn also liked to sit very low at the piano, just peering over the keyboard. It looked funny, but Glenn made great music that way, so who's to say it was wrong? Like most artists, Glenn Gould did things just a little bit differently than everyone else. But the same things that made Glenn different also made him great.

❧ Immanuel Kant ☙

A philosopher is someone who thinks for a living. Lots of people are paid to think about *one* thing, like money, or the weather. But a philosopher's job is to think about *everything*. They think about very hard questions, like: Does time have a beginning and an end? Does the world disappear when I close my eyes? Why am I me, and not somebody else? Some questions philosophers ask have more than one answer, or no answer at all. That's OK, because finding answers isn't really what we need philosophers for. What philosophers do for us is to help us find new ways to think.

Immanuel Kant grew up in a family of nine children. The Kants weren't wealthy, but they worked hard and were careful with their money. Immanuel learned to be very serious about whatever he did. He also learned that things like fancy clothes and big houses were not important. Those were part of the "outside" world, and Immanuel's family believed that what was on the inside was what really mattered. That stuck with Immanuel, and he became a philosopher, the most "inside" job there is.

All Immanuel really wanted to do was to read and think. But he had to make money to live on, too. So Immanuel taught university classes in the daytime and wrote at night. It was a lot of work! He managed to do it all because work was his life. Immanuel didn't have a wife or children and didn't spend his time on hobbies. What kept him going was his excitement at all the new ideas he had. In 1781, he published a book called *Critique of Pure Reason*. Finally, everyone else was able to find out what he was so excited about.

One thing Immanuel wrote about was the difference between the way things are and the way people think about them. For example: 2 + 2 = 4. Two rocks sitting next to two other rocks equals four rocks. This is always true, even if there are no humans around to see the rocks. But it took humans to think of the idea of two, and the idea of four, and the ideas of plus and equal. Without people, there would be no math. The rocks would just be rocks.

Did you understand that? If not, don't worry. Most people have a hard time getting Immanuel's ideas. But he wouldn't be famous if he only thought about easy questions. Immanuel wanted to make sense of the hardest questions he could think of. He did this by making his life simple, to give himself as much time as possible to think. Immanuel kept a very strict schedule every day, waking up at the same time, eating his meals at the same time, and working at the same time. His schedule was so precise that his neighbors set their watches by when he passed their houses on his daily walk. One day, Immanuel was so interested in a book he was reading that he skipped his walk to finish it. Everyone became confused, missing appointments and checking to see if their clocks had stopped. It was always remembered after that as the day Immanuel Kant didn't take his walk.

Barbara McClintock

Barbara McClintock was not your average kid. She would focus on something so hard that the rest of the world disappeared. Luckily, Barbara's parents didn't think it was important to be like everybody else. They wanted their children to learn on their own and they let them skip their homework—or even skip school!—to do it. Some kids might have used the time to goof off, but not Barbara. She became an independent thinker, whose greatest joy was discovery.

In college, Barbara learned about genes. Genes pass information from parents to their babies—or baby animals, or baby plants. They are what make you tall like your dad or a fast runner like your mom. Human genes are very complicated (scientists are still figuring them out today!); plant genes are much simpler. Barbara really wanted to figure out how genes worked, so she chose a plant that she felt would be easy to grow and easy to study. Barbara picked corn.

Barbara went on to teach while she was doing her corn research. Unfortunately, things weren't always easy at work. In Barbara's time, women were often paid less than men and treated badly on the job. Many women just did their best and pretended it didn't bother them. But Barbara could not pretend. Barbara was always true to herself, even if it meant not fitting in. In college, when other students were joining clubs called "sororities," Barbara was shocked to learn that these clubs kept some people out because of their religion. She didn't join, even though it was what everyone else was doing. Barbara knew she couldn't just go along.

And she knew she couldn't just go along with the way things were at work, either. Barbara quit her job. Before long, though, Barbara had a new job, a much better one. A friend invited her to come to a place called Cold Spring Harbor Research Center. It was a perfect place for Barbara. She had land to grow her corn, plenty of time to do her research, and, best of all, the respect she deserved. Barbara had found her place.

Barbara's discoveries were so far ahead of their time that it took 30 years for other scientists to realize how important they were. Barbara discovered how groups of genes—called "chromosomes"—could be told apart by their shape. She saw that chromosomes broke apart and stuck back together in new patterns. She did important work on mutations—how genes change so that "baby" plants can be different from their "parents." Things that Barbara discovered are still important today. But although she received many awards for her work, it wasn't until 1983—when she was 81 years old—that Barbara received the greatest honor of all: The Nobel Prize. Still, although she appreciated the award, all through the ceremony Barbara could only think of one thing: getting back home to her work.

❧ Joseph Cornell ❧

Some art is realistic—a painting of clouds, or a sculpture of a dog; some art is abstract—no picture, just colors, shapes, and textures; and some art is "surreal." Artists called surrealists try to express more than just what they see. Surrealism is about thoughts, dreams, and imagination. A surreal work of art might show a man with an apple for a head, or a woman crying jewel tears. The images can be strange, or even frightening. People who like surreal art like it because it gets deep inside them, into their memories and feelings. People who don't like surrealism don't like it for the same reason.

Surrealism got deep inside Joseph Cornell—and he liked it. Joseph was already an adult in the 1930s, but he still wasn't sure what he wanted to be. Then he saw a show of surreal art and was so inspired that he went home and made a collage. When the collage was done, Joseph took it back to the gallery where he'd seen the show. The owner loved Joseph's collage so much that he offered to show Joseph's work at his gallery. Finally, Joseph knew what he was. He was an artist.

Joseph needed things to make his collages with. So he spent his days visiting thrift stores and junk shops, sorting through piles of old magazines, maps, and photos. Little by little, Joseph started finding more than just pictures. He began to collect small objects, like birds' eggs, glasses, and marbles. The flat collages grew into three-dimensional "assemblages." Joseph built boxes for his objects out of wood and glass. Things that had seemed like trash before, like old dolls' heads and broken clocks, suddenly became beautifully sad. Joseph had a way of magically breathing life into things that other people threw away.

Although Joseph made surreal art, he wasn't one of the group of people who called themselves "The Surrealists." He knew some of them, but they didn't see him very often. For one thing, The Surrealists lived mostly in Europe. Joseph lived in New York and never traveled. Even if they had lived next door, though, Joseph probably wouldn't have spent his time with them. Joseph wasn't a party person. He liked taking long walks by himself, observing people and the city. Joseph did have friends who visited, but he preferred writing letters to hanging out.

Over the years, Joseph Cornell made a lot of art. Besides his collages and assemblages, he made surrealist films by cutting scenes together in a strange way. Joseph was also interested in music and dance, and he wrote for dance magazines. But he is best remembered for an art form that he made completely his own. Today, there are many artists still making deep wooden frames holding strange collections of objects. Each one is different, but what they share is the name of the man who made trash into treasures. They are called "Cornell Boxes."

❧ Hans Christian Andersen ❧

Hans Christian Andersen didn't fit in in his home town. So when he was just 14, he set out for the big city of Copenhagen. It was a very long walk, but Hans was excited. Soon he would be in a new place, where nobody knew him. Hans could start a brand new life!

Unfortunately, life in Copenhagen wasn't much better than it had been at home. Hans tried to find work but didn't have any luck. So instead he started school, but didn't fit in there, either. The other boys teased him for being tall and awkward, and they hurt his feelings. Even the teachers weren't very nice. Hans was sad, but he cheered himself up by writing stories. He wrote wonderful tales about mermaids and princes. In the 1830s, books were written in a formal style, using lots of long words. But Hans wrote simply, the way people really spoke. This was new to readers. His stories became very popular, both with kids and adults.

As Hans became famous, he started getting invitations to dances and dinner parties. Hans was pleased but worried, too. The people at these parties would be smart people, cool people, fancy people. How would he ever fit in? Despite his fears, Hans went to the parties. Slowly, he began to realize: His new friends didn't want him to fit in. They didn't invite Hans because he was like everyone else. They invited him because he was different. They invited him because he was interesting. They invited him because he was Hans.

Hans wrote about lots of different things, but one of his best-loved stories is about being different. *The Ugly Duckling* tells the story of a young duck who doesn't look or sound like everybody else. Just like Hans, he leaves home, looking for somewhere to belong—and just like Hans, he gets some bumps and bruises along the way. In the end though, the ugly duckling discovers that he's not ugly—he's not even a duckling! He's a beautiful swan. It took Hans a while, but he finally realized that just because he was different didn't mean there was something wrong with him. Hans had been a swan all along.

Hans Christian Andersen's stories have been read all over the world, and inspired everything from paintings to songs to movies. That sad 14-year-old boy long ago may have secretly hoped that he and his stories would some day be famous; but in his wildest dreams, he could not have guessed that a statue of one of his characters would watch over the harbor of the city he loved. In fact, today the Little Mermaid is the symbol of Copenhagen—the city where Hans feared he would never fit in.

ೞ Temple Grandin ಬ

Dr. Temple Grandin thinks like an animal. At least, she thinks the way she thinks an animal would think. Instead of thinking in words, she uses pictures. Temple has thousands of pictures stored in her head. When somebody says a word, she finds the picture that goes with it. When Temple wants to say something, she turns the pictures back into words.

Because of this ability, Temple and the animals she meets understand each other very well. One day, Temple met some very unhappy cows who were waiting to be vaccinated—a treatment that protects cows from becoming ill. They were afraid because people were making them walk through a scary walkway. The people didn't know that their walkway was scary, but Temple did. Cows don't like harsh lights and darks, and they don't like slippery floors. Temple designed a new facility that wasn't scary for cows. Since then, she has designed many facilities to be more animal-friendly. In appreciation of her work, the founder of an animal rights group once said that "Temple Grandin has done more to reduce suffering in the world than any other person who has ever lived." She also thought that, like cows, people might like to be squeezed. Some people like to be hugged when they feel afraid: It had always made Temple feel better. So she built a squeeze machine for people.

When Temple was a baby, in the 1940s, autism was not well known. Temple's mother wondered why her baby didn't like to be touched. She took Temple to a doctor. The doctor thought that something in Temple's brain was broken and could not be fixed. But Temple's mother didn't give up. She made sure that Temple had good teachers and lots of help. Temple worked very hard and did well in school. In college she earned a Ph.D. in animal science, and that is how she became Dr. Temple Grandin.

Today, Dr. Grandin has three jobs. Her first job is making the lives of animals better. Her second job is teaching students about animal science. Her third job is writing and speaking to groups of people about autism. These are three very important jobs, but best of all may be the job she does just by being herself: Temple Grandin is a role model for autistic people all over the world.

Wow, those people did a lot of great things! And they didn't let anybody else make them feel bad for not fitting in. They just turned what they did best into great art, or great inventions, or important new ideas. I still haven't decided what to do with my life—there's plenty of time for that! But whatever it is, I'm going to do it my own way, just like all the great people before me…only different.

Further Reading for Children

Albert Einstein
Brown, D. (2004) *Odd Boy Out: Young Albert Einstein*. Boston, MA: Houghton Mifflin.

Dian Fossey
Mathews, T.L. (1998) *Light Shining Through the Mist*. Washington, DC: National Geographic School Publishing.

Andy Warhol
Warhola, J. (2003) *Uncle Andy's*. New York, NY: Grosset & Dunlap.

Benjamin Banneker
Wadsworth, G. (2003) *Benjamin Banneker: Pioneering Scientist*. Minneapolis, MN: Lerner Publishing Group.

Andy Kaufman
Kaufman, A. (2000) *Soundstage: The Andy Kaufman Show* (video). Rhino Video.

Wassily Kandinsky
Rapelli, P. (1999) *Kandinsky: The Pioneer of a New Art Form*. New York, NY: Dorling Kindersley Publishing.

Julia Bowman Robinson
Reid, C. (1997) *Julia: A Life in Mathematics*. Washington, DC: The Mathematical Association of America.

Piet Mondrian
Faerna, J. M. (1997) *Mondrian Cameo (Great Modern Masters Series)*. New York, NY: Harry N Abrams.

Alan Turing
Hodges, A. (1999) *Turing (The Great Philosophers Series)*. Florence, KY: Routledge.

Sophie Germain
Reimer, L. and Reimer, W. (1990) *Mathematicians Are People, Too: Stories From the Lives of Great Mathematicians*. Parsippany, NJ: Dale Seymour Publications

Lewis Carroll
Bjork, C., Eriksson, I.K., and Sandin, J. (1993) *The Other Alice: The Story of Alice Liddell and Alice in Wonderland*. R & S Books

Nikola Tesla
Dommermuth-Costa, C. (1994) *Nikola Tesla: A Spark of Genius*. Minneapolis, MN: Lerner Publishing Group.

Paul Erdös
Pappas, T. (1993) *Fractals, Googols, and Other Mathematical Tales*. San Carlos, CA: Wide World Publishing.

Glenn Gould
Konieczny, V. (2004) *Struggling for Perfection: The Story of Glenn Gould*. Toronto, ON: Napoleon Publishing

Immanuel Kant
Weate, J. (1998) *Young Person's Guide to Philosophy*. New York, NY: Dorling Kindersley Publishing.

Barbara McClintock
Tracy, K. (2001) *Barbara McClintock: Pioneering Geneticist*. Hockessin, DE: Mitchell Lane Publishers.

Joseph Cornell
Cornell, J., Baverstock, A. and Wynne, C. (2003) *Secrets in a Box (Adventures in Art series).* New York, NY: Prestel Publishing.

Hans Christian Andersen
Yolen, J. and Nolan, D. (2005) *The Perfect Wizard: Hans Christian Andersen.* New York, NY: Dutton Juvenile.

Temple Grandin
Carpenter, M. (2003) *Rescued By a Cow and A Squeeze: Temple Grandin.* Frederick, MD: PublishAmerica

Further Reading for Adults and Advanced Readers

Baron-Cohen, S. (2003) *The Essential Difference: The Truth about the Male and Female Brain.* Philadelphia PA: Perseus Books Group.

Collins, P. (2005) *Not Even Wrong: A Father's Journey Into The Lost History of Autism.* New York, NY: Bloomsbury USA.

Fitzgerald, M. (2004) *Autism and Creativity: Is There a Link Between Autism in Men and Exceptional Ability?* New York, NY: Brunner-Routledge

Frith, U. (2003) *Autism: Explaining the Enigma.* Oxford: Blackwell Publishing.

Grandin, T., and Johnson, C. (2005) *Animals in Translation: Using the Mysteries of Autism to Decode Animal Behavior.* New York, NY: Scribner.

Houston, R.A., and Frith, U. (2000) *Autism in History: The Case of Hugh Blair of Borgue.* Oxford: Blackwell Publishing.

Paradiž, V. (2005) *Elijah's Cup: A Family's Journey Into the Community and Culture of High-Functioning Autism and Asperger's Syndrome.* London: Jessica Kingsley Publishers.

Of related interest

Blue Bottle Mystery
An Asperger Adventure
Kathy Hoopmann
ISBN 978 1 85302 978 3

Of Mice and Aliens
An Asperger Adventure
Kathy Hoopmann
ISBN 978 0 85700 179 5

Buster and the Amazing Daisy
Nancy Ogaz
ISBN 1 84310 721 X

What Did You Say? What Do You Mean?
An Illustrated Guide to Understanding Metaphors
Jude Welton
ISBN 978 1 84310 721 7

Different Croaks for Different Folks
All About Children with Special Learning Needs
Midori Ochiai
With notes on developmental differences by Shinya Miyamoto
Illustrated by Hiroko Fujiwara
Translated by Esther Sanders
ISBN 978 1 84310 392 9